The BE A PINEAPPLE

STAND TALL,
WEAR A CROWN,
& BE SWEET ON THE INSIDE

Adult Coloring Book

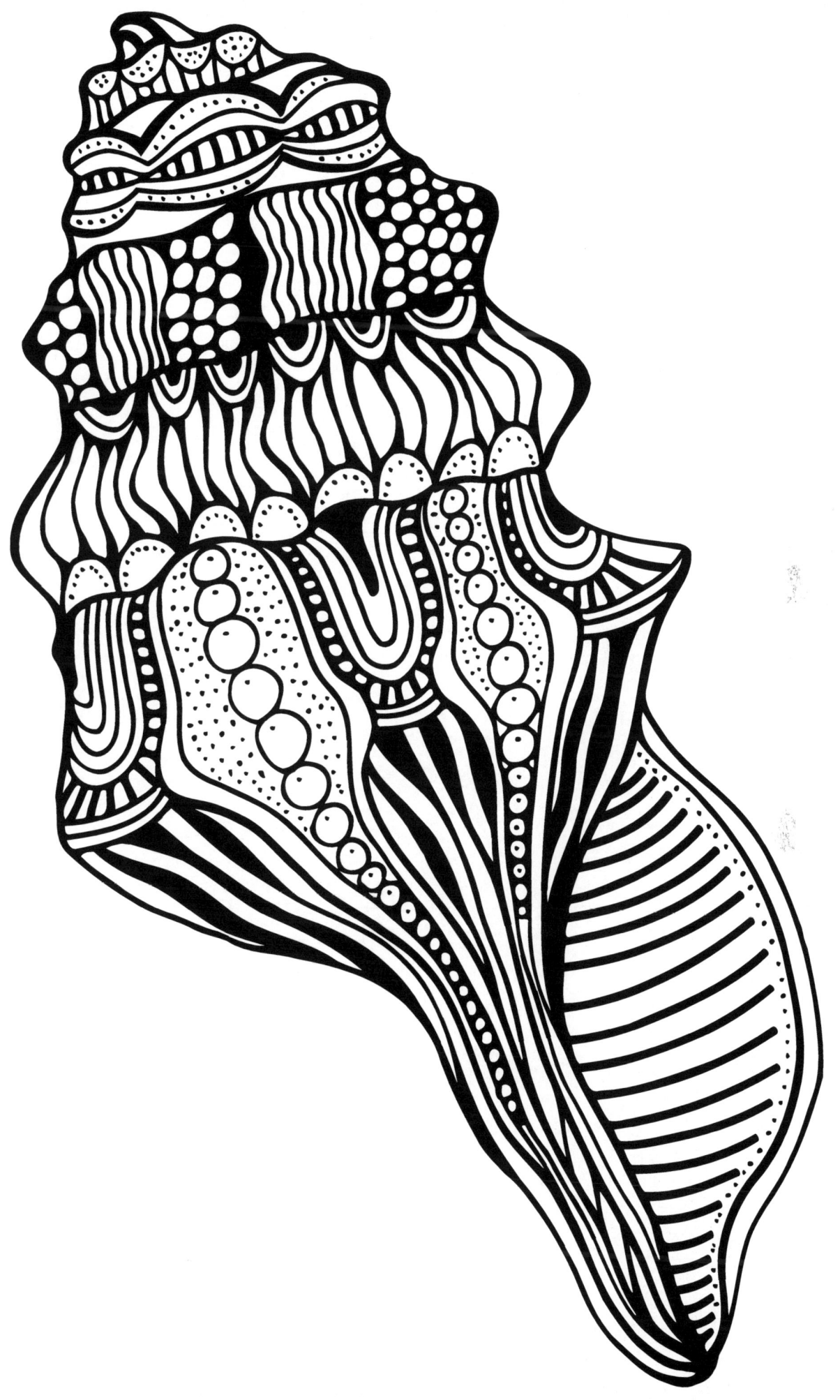

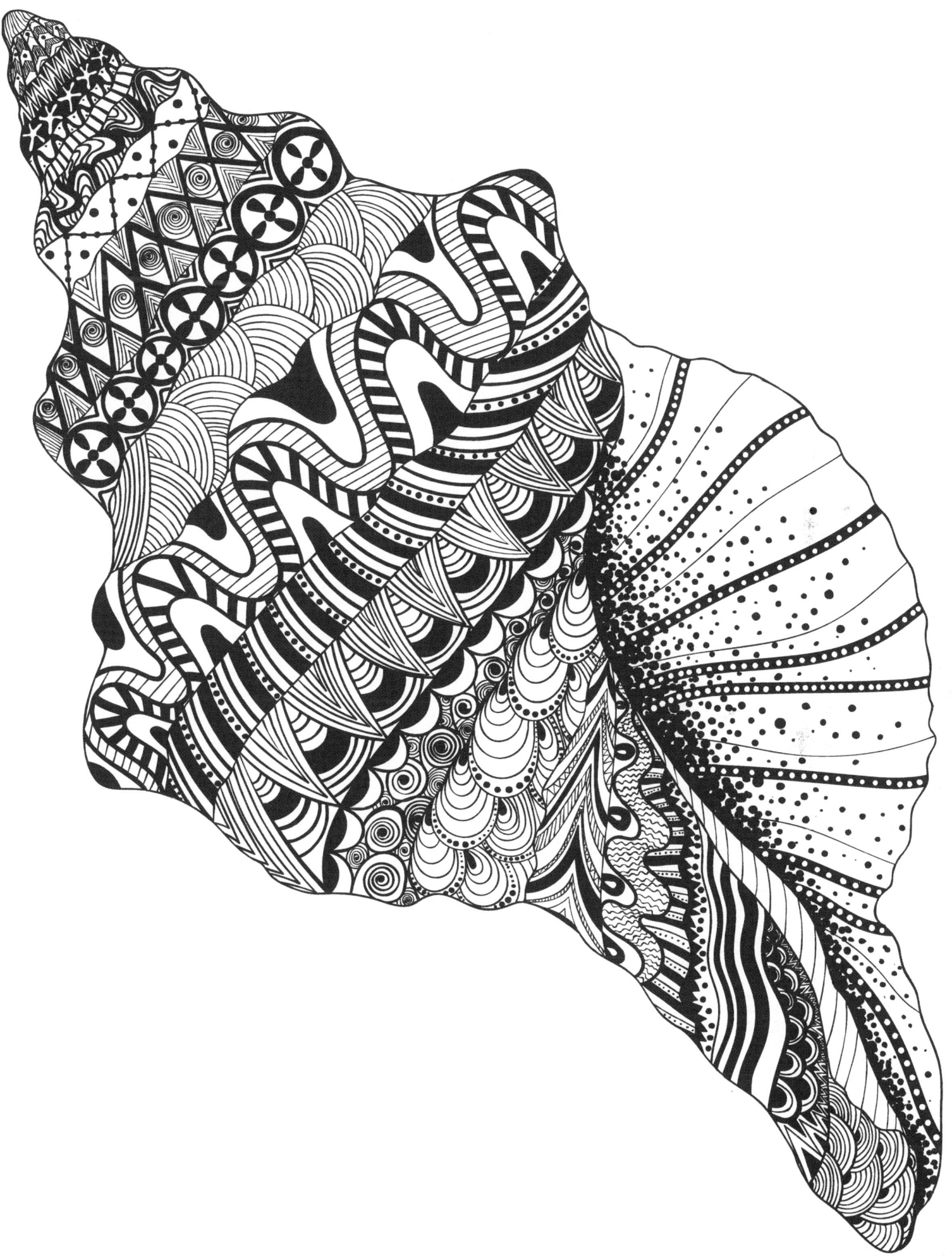

Color Test Page

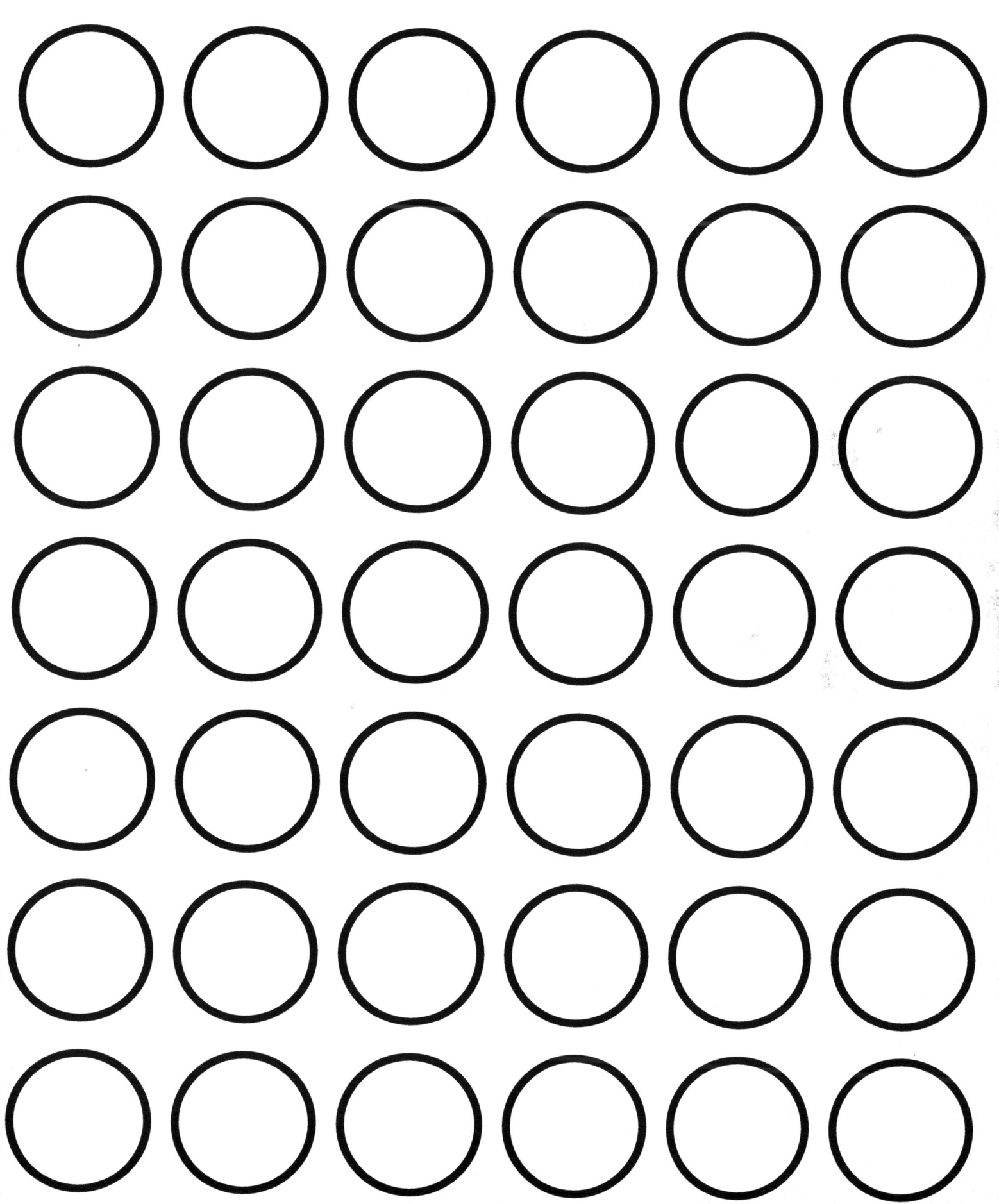

For more amazing journals and adult coloring books from RW Squared Media, visit:

Amazon.com
CreateSpace.com
RWSquaredMedia.Wordpress.com

She Believed She Could
So She Did
Adult Coloring Book

Start Where You Are
Adult Coloring Book

Cities of the World
Coloring Book for Adults

The Low Carb, Gluten Free,
Vegetarian Coloring Book
for Adults

Be A Pineapple
Stand Tall
Wear A Crown
and Be Sweet On the Inside
Notebook

She Believed She Could So She
Did Journal for Women
(with adult coloring mandalas)

BONUS!!!

Link to download free PDF version of
"Color Your Butterflies Away"

https://RWSquaredMedia.wordpress.com/free-coloring-book/

For inspirational prints and posters, visit:

https://InspirationalWares.com

Printed in Great Britain
by Amazon